COOKING FOR THE
NEW MARS

COOKING FOR THE
NEW MARS

By Margaret Ellory

bushi-go, inc

Text copyright © 2015 by bushi-go, inc.
Illustrations copyright © 2015 by bushi-go, inc.

All rights reserved. No part of this book may be reproduced in any form without written permission except in the case of brief quotations embodied in critical articles and reviews.

www.cookingforthenewmars.com

FIRST EDITION

Library of Congress Cataloging-in-Publication Data:

Ellory, Margaret
    Cooking for the New Mars / by Margaret Ellory – 1st ed.
    ISBN 978-0-9970793-0-2
    1. Science – space. 2. Cookery – dehydrated.
    3. Food – Experiments.   I. Ellory, Margaret. II. Title

bushi-go, inc.
32 Valley View
San Mateo, California 94403

*To M, L, M and C,
because yes, you have to eat that.*

CONTENTS

Introduction – 11
Imported or Local – 15
Protein Sources – 19
Grains and Oils – 23
Fruits – 24
The Absent – 27
Constraints – 29

MEALWORM

Patties – 33
Tacos – 35
Meatballs – 36
Martian Fudge – 39
Candied Mealworms – 41

CUY

Cuy and Vegetable Stew – 43
Cuy Quinoa – 45
Burgers – 47
Meatloaf – 49
Roasted Cuy – 51

CARP

Patties – 53
Chowder – 55
Tacos – 57
Roasted – 59
Hash – 61

QUAIL

Roasted – 63
Quail and Quinoa Soup – 65
Quail Tacos – 67
Quail Cobb Salad – 69
Quail Broth – 71

VEGETARIAN

Curry Potatoes – 73
Mushroom Crepes – 75
Mushroom Quinoa – 77
Borscht – 79
Zucchini pancakes – 81
Candied Beets – 83

MISC

Tortillas – 85
Beet Syrup – 87
Flour – 89
Catsup – 91
Sweet Potato Bread – 92
Beet Wine – 94
Beet Vinegar – 97
Salsa - 99

ERRATA

Dehydrated Foods – 100
Altitude Issues – 103
Notes on Husbandry – 107
The New Ecology – 109
References – 111
Acknowledgements – 113
About the Author – 114

INTRODUCTION

The kitchen is the soul of the home. I don't care if you're a handful of cowboys punching steer in a Wyoming spring or New York socialite trying to impress her in-laws, the preparation of food and the meal that follows after serve an integral, psychological function in our lives.

Right now when it comes to travel in space we are often more familiar with the mechanics of preparation. How do we keep peas out of the CO^2 filter? How do we avoid getting the toggle switches sticky with maple syrup thumb-prints. How can we combat food boredom? How do we deliver enough nutrients to keep a person healthy in a minimum of space. We can make foods barely tasty enough, ensconced in their carefully weighted foil pouches, but we have a much harder time mimicking the satisfaction you feel when you present the first pan of scrambled eggs you didn't burn, or the look on your lover's face the first time she tries your grandmother's famous pecan pie.

Cooking for the New Mars is not concerned with near orbit stuff, the issue of weightlessness or total lack of atmosphere do not arise the same way when cooking on the surface of any planet. This book is for the reconstitution of the soul, for thoughts on the creation of new recipes and new techniques that will invariably evolve as we begin the colonization of our sister world. I want to look at necessary substitutions, potential evolutionary steps and try to find ways to involve existing well known recipes so that they fit theoretical conditions. This involves some tweaking of the tools, some adaptation for ways and means of preparation. Some of the groundwork has been laid already not only by the genius food engineers across the world who develop menus and foodstuffs that are currently in use in space, but also those who travel in extreme situations. Arctic backpackers, doomsday preppers, marathoners, campers who need to carry a maximum amount of calories in a minimum amount of space on their backs for an extended period of time. The research has been done, we just need to get off planet to really put it through its paces.

Cooking adapts over time, cooking changes with the people who do the preparation. As humankind spread out across our blue planet, ingredients changed, techniques evolved and tastes adapted depending on what was available. Different foods were in season, different animals were discovered and made it onto the menu. Recipes from the home country depended on what could be traded, bartered for or imported. This very human tendency to adapt and personalize new lives to new environments is the kind of thing we will have to plan for as we move off-planet to new worlds.

In the psychology of food preparation, Mars will be no different than the colonization of any other continent in the history of mankind. We will take with us the memories of home, the small tastes and touches that can survive the journey and nourish the soul, but once we touch down everything is going to have to change.

I can't wait to see what we come up with.

IMPORTED OR LOCAL

For the purposes of this cookbook I'm categorizing foods along very simple guidelines. You're either going to have locally grown foods and imports.

Things that we can grow on Mars gives us our *local foods*. Whether or not we can is not much of a question, we are *really* good at growing things. We can grow foods on the space station right now, and have, in fact, been working out the details of growing foods in space/offworld for decades. We have experience developing foods that can be produced in a very limited space with limited resources. Some of these are engineered foods (GMOs) some are not.

We also have to take usage into consideration. For example, growing nothing but kale, while it may seem healthy for a time, is going to eventually give you nutrient-poor soil, the kind that will not grow much of anything. In addition, nutrients and growing "seasons" will need to be taken into account. Ideally you will have multiple growing areas along with multiple crops in rotation, each of which can provide not only foods for the humans to use, but wastes that can be put back into the soil in order to provide nutrients for the next crop.

We have an advantage in that farming will take place in a controlled space. We set the night/day cycles. We get to decide the timing of the growing seasons.

Imported foods, in contrast, are going to be the foodstuffs we either bring with us or have delivered via supply run. Don't kid yourself, there will be supply runs for as long as we can possibly make them happen. While, in theory, we could ship anything from pre-packaged t-bone steaks to escargot and vino, shipping is going to be prohibitively expensive, and will probably be restricted to absolute needs as much as possible.

Imported foods (presumably from Earth) will be marked in the recipies as *(i)* and local foods will be marked as *(l)*. In some cases (like oils and eggs) you might have both available and what you use will be a matter of personal taste rather than availability.

LIST OF IMPORTS

DEHYDRATED BUTTER
POWDERED MILK
DEHYDRATED EGG WHITE
DEHYDRATED EGG YOLK
MOTHER OF VINEGAR
TUMERIC
CUMIN
CINNAMON
PEPPER
BAY
TACO SEASONING
CHEESE POWDER
CORIANDER
PAPRIKA
DEHYDRATED ONION
DRIED ANCHO CHILIES
GARLIC POWDER

PROTEIN SOURCES

Getting bacon to Mars, while entirely within the bounds of human capability, is going to take a lot of time and effort. Bacon is going to be the Dom Pérignon of the New Mars. I find this a fine idea and a tragedy all at the same time.

There are no native animals on Mars, there is no native biology at all that we have discovered so far. So any animals will have to be brought with us. This not only limits the selection, but it also requires us to define our usage of those animals. In many cases they may be valuable for reasons other than just consumption.

We take mice into space all the time for experimentation. Mice breed like crazy and can be quite tasty if prepared well. If you are breeding mice as experimental subjects, any overflow can get rolled into the protein supply.

Alternatively we can use something a little bit larger but that breeds almost as fast. Cuy, or guinea pigs are already used as a primary source of animal protein. You get larger more satisfying pieces of meat to work with than with mice or rats. They make fine companions and are less likely to get into the wiring and chew holes in your walls if they escape. In addition, their poop has nitrogen-fixing properties that can aid in plant fertilization and nutrition.

Mealworms are another excellent source of protein. Small size means that they are easier to use as an additive then as a main dish. You can cook them up and munch them like popcorn, you can grind them into a powder and use them as a protein supplement in your milkshakes or your soups. They can serve as a disposal method, converting scraps of edible matter too small for humans to take advantage of back into an ongoing protein source.

Next, let's think about fish. Easy to transport, freshwater fish like cod can be frozen in an embryonic stage then allowed to grow to maturity once your reach Mars. They can work very well with hydroponic systems, helping to provide nutrients to the plants and helping to keep the tanks free of algae.

The foul may be a little bit tricky, but quail have already been successfully raised and maintained in a zero-g atmosphere, and the embryos could be frozen for the long trip to Mars. Quail provide meat, eggs (small ones, but still vital for baking) as well as feces that are an excellent source of nitrogen for growing plants.

There are vegan and vegetarian protein options as well, the plant we selected as our "oil-bearing" option produces protein heavy cakes as part of the oil production process. These can be ground and used as protein supplements.

We also elected to include one of the "meatier" families of mushrooms as one of our potential plant options, not only because they can help to make filling dishes when meat is not an option, but because they are valuable as culinary additives to other dishes as well as providing another good use for organic compost.

LIST OF PROTEINS

CUY

QUAIL

MEALWORMS

QUAIL EGGS

OILSEED

QUINOA

CARP

GRAINS AND OILS

So many recipes depend on grains, not just to make soft, fluffy breads and tasty chocolate chip cookies, but as thickeners and as binding agents. The problem is that grains are space intensive. In order to get enough to be useful, we need to grow a lot. With an eye towards multiple-uses, I've narrowed down a few that could be cultivated in small quantities (hull-less oats being our list item), but keep in mind that, for starters, these kinds of ingredients are going to need to go solidly into the "imports" category, to be used sparingly.

In a similar vein, oils are most easily derived from animal fats, but we do have a plant on our list that can provide not only the oil we need for cooking, but a hefty dose of protein plus they can be turned into a suitable flour for vegan and vegetarian options.

FRUITS

Imports only, sorry.

LIST OF PLANTS

ZUCCHINI
BEETS
ROMAINE LETTUCE
OILSEED
PORTOBELLO MUSHROOMS
CARROTS
CELERY
SWEET POTATOES
WHITE POTATOES
SHALLOTS
HULL-LESS OATS
TOMATOES
QUINOA
BASIL
CILANTRO
DULSE (BACON ALGAE)

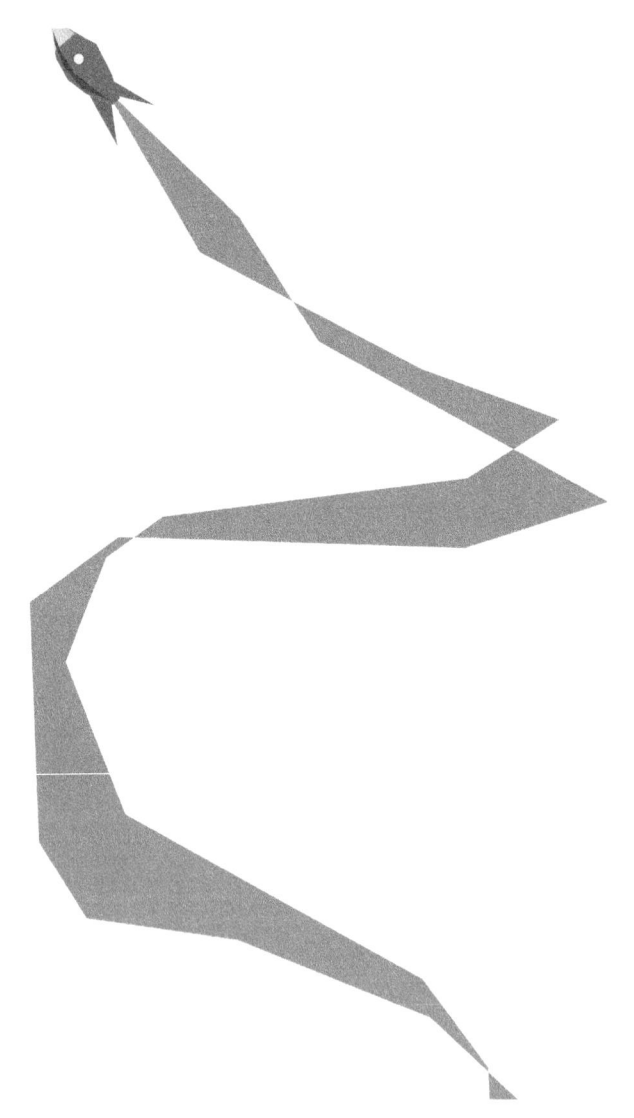

THE ABSENT

You may have noticed by looking through the ingredient lists provided here and my thoughts on different types of small-scale food production that there is one glaring piece of humankind's diet missing.

Dairy.

There are two ways to look at this. Right now production of dairy products requires an animal that produces milk. While it is not beyond imagination that we could develop a process to produce milk via other methods, I haven't been able to find much in the way of non-mammalian milk.

There are milk and cheese substitutes out there and all of these are produced without the involvement of a mammal other than a human scientist. Their nutritional profiles are different than dairy. Protein levels are different, fiber levels are different, calcium levels are different, most of the nutritional content has been engineered to approach dairy milk. In the cases of almond milk, soy milk and vegetarian cheeses, their primary function is to serve as a non-dairy substitute ingredient, rather than standalone non-dairy substitute (soy milk on your cereal, for example). Producing any of the substitute products is as resource intensive as raising a cow or a goat, so the current production methods are not going to help us much when it comes to substituting for milk on Mars.

Select vegetables and other foods can help make up for the lack in protein, calcium and fats. Unless we can find a truly bioengineered option (like milk from re-engineered e-coli) its not clear that raising cattle or goats or camels or mares is going to make a lot of sense on a place like Mars. There have been inroads into making novelty milk products using human breast milk, so that is always an option, but that requires our female settlers to be pregnant. It would likely be a later stage product, an individual product (much like sauerkraut or yogurt is produced by an individual's household in parts of the world, rather than bought in a shop) produced after the settlers began having children.

CONSTRAINTS

The tools you have to cook with are going to make a difference on Mars. Open flame elements, like barbeques and broilers are pretty much right out. In an off-world habitat you are going to have a limited, constantly circulated air supply. That means that all of the smells you put into the air are going to stay there. That includes the bad ones. And, as anyone who has ever tried to fix stinky sweat-socks by dumping perfume onto them knows, sometimes it is just better to adapt to the smell than to try an improve upon it.

Everything is likely going to need to be heated through various induction, convection or conductive methods. Frying/browning is going to be tricky unless a specialized piece of equipment is involved, so these recipes have been adapted to be cooked appropriately.

As anyone who has lived off the land for any period of time, either deliberately or not, can attest to, single-use cooking tools are not always desireable. You end up with a single "Old Reliable" after a while and use that to prepare all kinds of experimental dishes. Add to that the constraints of shipping through space and you have a deep need for "multi-use tools".

Much like the foodstuffs, everything needs to serve more than one purpose. A small convection oven, for example, can be used not only to cook food for immediate consumption, but it could be used to dry products for storage and even be used (with great care) for scientific equipment prep. (though you're probably going to want to be extra careful nobody mistakes the mold-growth experiment for a late-night snack of baked kale).

Recipes with similar ingredients should be able to be cooked with different tools (so, for example, we don't want to have a food product that can *only* be cooked in the convection oven, because if that oven breaks down you're going to have trouble).

LIST OF TOOLS

ELECTRIC CONVECTION OVEN

MICROWAVE OVEN

HOT PLATE/ELECTRIC STOVETOP

OIL PRESS

GRINDER

CROCK POT

Mealworm Patties

2 cups chopped fresh mealworm *(l)*
½ cup shredded zucchini *(l)*
1 tbsp oil *(l)*
½ cup oilseed flour *(l)*
¼ cup dehydrated onion flakes *(l)*
½ cup egg (reconstituted) *(i)*
Salt and pepper to taste *(i/l)*

Do not pre-cook the mealworms. Place them outside for 12 minutes, then allow to thaw before chopping. Mix all ingredients and form into balls roughly the size of golf-balls. Sprinkle with water if necessary.

Press into patties and place in pan. Cook in convection oven for 5 minutes, then turn and cook the other side. Brown the patties on both sides. Be sure patties have been cooked through to the middle.

Serves 6-8

Let's face it, you are going to be stuck with a very small community of people for quite a long time.

These "Small Talk" panels are intended to be conversation starters for when things get a little too "same old/same old".

SMALL TALK

Mealworm Tacos

1 cup fresh mealworms *(l)*
2 tbsp taco seasoning *(i)*
1 tbsp butter powder *(i)*
6 tortillas *(l)*

Shredded lettuce *(l)*
Cheese powder (reconstituted) *(i)*
Salsa *(l)*

Do not pre-cook the mealworms. Place them outside for 12 minutes, then allow to thaw. Toss with taco seasoning and butter powder. Wrap in foil or enclose in a cooking container. Bake for 15 min at 350 degrees. Allow to cool.

Wrap in tortillas and serve with optional ingredients to taste.

Serves 4-6

Just how high CAN you jump out on the Martian surface? Have you tried? Can you jump higher now than when you first arrived?

SMALL TALK

Mealworm Meatballs

2 cups veg-fed mealworm *(l)*
1 tbsp oil *(l)*
½ cup oilseed flour *(l)*
¼ cup dehydrated onion flakes *(l)*
½ cup egg (reconstituted) *(i)*
Salt and pepper to taste *(i/l)*

Mix all ingredients and form into balls roughly the size of golf-balls. Mixture should be moist enough to hold together, but not soggy.

Press into patties and place in pan. Cook in convection oven for 5 minutes, then turn and cook the other side. The oilseed should provide enough oil to brown the patties on both sides. Be sure patties have been cooked through to the middle.

Serves 6-8

Everybody was able to bring some personal items from home, but by now they may be wearing thin. If you could trade one item with anybody else, what item would you trade and why?

SMALL TALK

Martian Fudge

¾ cup roasted, mashed beets *(l)*
¾ cup beet syrup *(l)*
½ cup oilseed butter *(l)*
¼ cup powdered milk (reconstituted) *(i)*
2 tsp powdered butter *(i)*
1 cup mealworm flour *(l)*
½ cup oat flour *(l)*
Vanilla *(i)*

Mix mashed beets, beet syrup, oilseed butter, milk, butter powder and vanilla.

Slowly add mealworm flour and oat flour until you get a thick cookie-like dough.

Spread in a pan, cover and place outside the habitat for around 15 minutes. Slice into bars and enjoy.

Makes 1 dozen

Is there a story from your experiences you want to see pass forward and become a Martian folk tale? What is it?

SMALL TALK

Candied Mealworms

2 cups beet fed mealworms *(l)*
1 cup beet syrup *(l)*
1 tsp cinnamon (optional) *(i)*
1 tsp oil *(l)*
1/8 cup rehydrated egg white *(i)*
1 tsp Salt *(l)*

Place mealworms outside the habitat for about 15 minutes until stiff.

Mix eggs and oil until slightly foamy. Toss mealworms in mixture until well coated. Add sugar and cinnamon and toss until all the worms are thoroughly coated.

Toast in oven at 250 degrees for about 30 minutes or until lightly browned and dry.

Serves 1 (because you will not want to share)

Cuy and Vegetable Stew

3 cups boiling water *(l)*
1 ½ cup cubed cuy meat *(l)*
½ cup celery *(l)*
½ cup carrots *(l)*
½ cup oat flour *(l)*
1 tbsp chopped shallots *(l)*
4 tbsp stewed tomato *(l)*
Salt and pepper to taste *(l/i)*

Pour boiling water over cuy meat and allow to simmer for 1 hour, checking occasionally as water reduces. Add vegetables and simmer for another 30 minutes. Add flour, cook until thickened. Salt and pepper to taste.

Serves 6-8

What's the strangest food combination you've tried while here on Mars? Why did that seem like a good idea at the time?

SMALL TALK

Cuy Quinoa

2 cups quinoa *(l)*
6 tbsp chopped shallot *(l)*
1 tsp ground coriander *(i)*
1 tsp ground cumin *(i)*
1 tsp ground paprika *(i)*
1 cup cubed, roasted cuy meat *(l)*
2 cups water *(l)*
Salt and pepper to taste *(l/i)*

Bring water to a boil in the microwave. Combine all dry ingredients and slowly add to boiling water. Put back in the microwave for 5 minutes or until quinoa is tender. Add cuy cubes and place in oven for 20 minutes at 350 degrees to heat through.

Serves 4

Have you noticed any new or changed colloquialisms popping up? Like saying, "Why on Mars..." instead of "Why on Earth..." Have you consciously made any new ones?

SMALL TALK

Cuy Burgers

2 cups minced or ground cuy *(l)*
1/2 cup egg *(l)*
1/4 cup oilseed flour *(l)*
Salt and pepper to taste *(l/i)*

Mix all ingredients and form into balls roughly the size of golf-balls. Mixture should be moist enough to hold together, but not soggy.

Press into patties and place in pan. Cook in convection oven for 5 minutes, then turn and cook the other side. The oilseed flour should provide enough oil to brown the patties on both sides. Be sure patties have been cooked through, with no pink in the middle.

Serves 6-8

How do you all decide on names for new discoveries? Discoverer's choice? Committee? Do you have a name you're just WAITING to use on something cool?

SMALL TALK

Cuy Meatloaf

2 cups minced cuy *(l)*
1 tortilla, shredded *(l)*
½ cup egg (quail or reconstituted) *(l/i)*
1 cup shallot, chopped fine *(l)*
½ cup milk (reconstituted) *(i)*
4 tbsp catsup *(l)*
1 tsp ground bay leaves *(i)*
1 tsp salt *(l)*

Combine all ingredients and mix well. Place in a loaf pan and cook at 350 degrees for 1 hour.

Mix and heat ½ cup catsup and 4 tbsp beet syrup and serve on the side.

Serves 6

It takes a while to shuttle information back and forth to Earth. Has the information infrastructure on Mars begun to grow? Who designed your internet? Does it talk to Earth's Internet?

SMALL TALK

Roasted Cuy

2-4 cuy, cut into pieces *(l)*
1 cup shallots, minced *(l)*
¼ cup garlic podwer *(i)*
1 tsp cumin *(i)*
3 tbsp oil *(i)*
1 tsp ground bay leaves *(i)*
1 tsp salt *(l)*

Combine all ingredients and mix well. Coat cuy pieces and allow to marinate in the mixture overnight.

Roast in oven at 350 degrees for 30 minutes, basting with oil frequently to avoid drying out the meat.

Serves 4-8

Carp Patties

2 cups flaked, roasted carp *(l)*
1 tbsp oil *(l)*
½ cup oilseed flour *(l)*
¼ cup minced shallots *(l)*
½ cup egg (reconstituted or quail) *(i/l)*
2 tbsp chopped beet greens *(l)*
Salt and pepper to taste *(i/l)*

Mix all ingredients and form into balls roughly the size of golf-balls. Sprinkle with water if necessary.

Press into patties and place in pan. Cook in convection oven for 5 minutes, then turn and cook the other side. Brown the patties on both sides. Be sure patties have been cooked through to the middle.

Serves 6-8

There are always extra corners and pockets of space in any structure. Have you found any secret hiding places? What did you hide in there?

SMALL TALK

Carp Chowder

2 cups uncooked carp cubes *(l)*
½ cup chopped celery *(l)*
½ cup minced beet greens *(l)*
1 cup vegetable broth *(l)*
2 tbsp butter powder *(i)*
1 tsp ground bay leaves *(i)*
½ cup oat flour *(l)*
Salt and pepper to taste *(l/i)*

Simmer carp, celery, beet greens, carrots and bay leaves in broth for 30 minutes. Add butter and oat flour and cook for another 20 minutes to thicken. Salt and pepper to taste.

Serves 4-6

Entertainment is as necessary in its own way as sleeping and eating. What's your favorite thing to do for fun?

SMALL TALK

Carp Tacos

1 large carp cut into sections *(l)*
2 tbsp taco seasoning *(i)*
1 tbsp butter powder
6 tortillas *(l)*

Optional:
Shredded lettuce *(l)*
Minced shallots *(l)*
Minced cilantro *(l)*
Cheese powder (reconstituted) *(i)*
Salsa *(l)*

Mix taco seasoning and butter powder well. Rub all over carp. Wrap in foil or enclose in a cooking container. Bake for 30 min at 350 degrees. Allow to cool, then flake carp with a fork. Wrap in tortillas and serve with optional ingredients to taste.

Serves 4-6

Who makes your clothes? Do you get them shipped, as is, from Earth? Do you think Mars needs to develop its own fashion sense?

SMALL TALK

Roasted Carp

1 large carp cut into sections *(l)*
½ tsp salt *(l)*
¼ cup grated shallot (white part) *(l)*
2 tbsp chopped cilantro *(l)*
1 tbsp butter powder *(i)*

Mix parsley, onion and butter powder into a paste and rub all over carp. Sprinkle salt on carp and wrap in foil or enclose in a cooking container. Bake for 30 min at 350 degrees.

Serves 4-6

Do you know someone who collects small rocks? Maybe someone who builds cityscapes out of MRE packages? What kind of creative repurposing have you done?

SMALL TALK

Carp Hash

2 cups roasted carp *(l)*
1 cup chopped shallots *(l)*
½ cup chopped celery *(l)*
½ cup chopped beet greens *(l)*
2 cups sliced mushrooms *(l)*
1 tbsp butter powder *(i)*
3 tbsp oil *(l)*
Salt and pepper to taste

Mix shallots, celery, beet greens, mushrooms, butter powder and oil in a pan and roast in 350 degree oven until onions are transparent. Stir in roasted carp and cook until brown, stirring frequently.

Serves 6

Roasted Quail

4 whole, cleaned and plucked quail *(l)*
2 sticks of celery *(l)*
2 carrots *(l)*
2 whole shallots *(l)*
1 tbsp butter powder *(i)*
3 tbsp oil *(l)*
Salt and pepper to taste *(l/i)*

Whip butter powder and oil together until slightly foamy and coat the quail, inside and out. Place quail, breast side up, in a shallow roasting pan. Cut celery sticks and use them to prop up the quail so they don't roll over. Fill Quail body cavity with remaining celery, shallots and carrot.

Roast at 500 degrees for 15 minutes.

Serves 4

Did you solve a problem today? How'd it go? Big problem, small problem, personal problem, engineering problem?

SMALL TALK

Quail Tacos

4 whole, cleaned, plucked and deboned quail *(l)*
3 cups of salsa *(l)*
6 tortillas *(l)*

Optional:
Shredded lettuce *(l)*
Minced shallots *(l)*
Minced cilantro *(l)*
Cheese powder (reconstituted) *(i)*

Roast quail in 350 degree oven until cooked through. Place quail in a covered pan with salsa and continue to cook in the oven at 350 degrees for 15 minutes. Once cooked, pull meat gently apart with a fork.

Wrap in tortillas and serve with optional ingredients to taste.

Serves 4-6

What's your favorite local food here on Mars? How about your least? Are there any new foods on the horizon that you are really excited about? Are there any new ones you think you should try cultivating?

SMALL TALK

Quail and Quinoa Soup

2 cups shredded, roasted quail *(l)*
1 cup quail broth *(l)*
3 cups water *(l)*
2 carrots, chopped large *(l)*
1 cup celery, chopped *(l)*
½ cup shallots, chopped *(l)*
½ cup beet greens, chopped *(l)*
1 tbsp cilantro, chopped *(l)*
1 cup quinoa *(l)*
Salt and pepper to taste *(l/i)*

Toss carrots, celery, shallots and beet greens with oil and roast until soft and slightly browned. Transfer to a pot and add quinoa, broth and salt to taste. Bring to a boil, then reduce heat and cover until quinoa softens. Add quail and cook until warm through.

Serves 4 - 6

Any ideas about how to create building materials on a planet without any organic resources? (Giant, carve-able crystals? New kind of plastics from the plants you grow?)

SMALL TALK

Quail Cobb Salad

4 roasted quail, deboned and chopped *(l)*
1/4 cup chopped dulse *(l)*
½ cup chopped tomatoes *(l)*
½ cup chopped celery *(l)*
½ cup shredded carrots *(l)*

4 cups of lettuce, torn and plated *(l)*
½ cup beet vinegar *(l)*
¼ cup oilseed oil *(l)*

Vigorously mix oil and vinegar until blended.

Toss all ingredients except lettuce in a bowl, add 2 tbsp oil and vinegar mix and continue to toss until coated.

Spoon vegetable and quail mixture over lettuce. Serve with a side dish of the oil and vinegar dressing.

Serves 4

Have you ever thought about making your own movies here on Mars? What style of movie would you want to make? Western? Musical? Should Mars have its own, unique style? What do you think it should be called?

SMALL TALK

Quail Broth

4 quail carcasses *(l)*
1 cup shallots, chopped large *(l)*
6 carrots, sliced *(l)*
6 celery sticks, cut in half *(l)*
1 tsp powdered bay leaves *(i)*
½ cup chopped beet greens *(l)*
1 tbsp powdered garlic *(i)*
1 gallon water *(l)*

Bring water to a boil and add all ingredients. Bring to a boil, then reduce to a simmer. Simmer for 6 hours, skimming the surface regularly. Add water as needed to keep all ingredients submerged.

Strain out solids and refrigerate overnight (do not place outside, we need the fat to rise to the top and separate). Remove fat and store.

Serves 6-8

Curry Potatoes

2 cups boiled potatoes *(l)*
1 cup boiling water *(l)*
2 tbsp powdered butter *(l)*
2 tbsp quail broth *(l)*
2 tsp chopped shallot *(l)*
1 tsp turmeric (or curry powder) *(i)*
Salt and pepper to taste *(l/i)*

Bring water to a boil on the hot plate. Combine all ingredients well and add to water, boil for about 2 minutes.

Pour boiling water over the potatoes and mash with a fork until fluffy.

Serves 6-8

Did you bring any habits from home that have worked out really well? What about ones you had to break because they were causing problems for you?

SMALL TALK

Mushroom Crepes

2 cups egg (quail or reconstituted) *(l/i)*
1 tsp reconstituted milk *(i)*
1 cup protein powder *(l)*
2 tbsp powdered butter *(i)*
1 cup chopped beet greens *(l)*
1 cup chopped mushrooms *(l)*

Toss mushrooms and beet greens with powdered butter. Cover and microwave for 1 minute. Set aside.

Whip egg and milk together until slightly foamy. Slowly add protein powder. Mixture should be runny, not stiff. Cook in a nonstick pan on a hot-plate until the surface is bubbly. Flip and cook the other side until light brown.

Ladle mushroom/spinach mixture over crepes and serve.

Serves 4-6

The seasons on Mars are totally different from the seasons on Earth. Don't you think they should have their own (safe to be uttered in polite company) names? Would that get too confusing?

SMALL TALK

Mushroom Quinoa

2 cups quinoa *(l)*
6 tbsp chopped shallot *(l)*
1 tsp ground coriander *(i)*
1 tsp ground cumin *(i)*
1 tsp ground paprika *(i)*
2 cups diced mushrooms *(l)*
2 cups water *(l)*
Salt and pepper to taste *(l/i)*

Bring water to a boil on the hot plate. Combine all dry ingredients and slowly add to boiling water. Simmer until quinoa is tender, drain. Toss with mushrooms and place in oven for 15 minutes at 350 degrees to heat through.

Serves 4

Mac or PC? Which one do you think will become the new Martian standard? Something new maybe?

SMALL TALK

Borscht

2 tbsp oil *(l)*
2 cups vegetable broth *(l)*
2 large potatoes, peeled and diced *(l)*
1 carrot, sliced *(l)*
1 ½ cups beet root, cubed and steamed until tender *(l)*
1 cup chopped shallot (white) *(l)*
1 tsp garlic *(i)*
Salt and pepper to taste *(l/i)*

Coat onion, potato and carrot in oil. Sprinkle with garlic and roast in oven until tender and just brown. Transfer to a pot and add broth, salt and pepper, bring to a boil. Add beets and cook until the broth is deep red and the potatoes are very soft.

Serves 6-8

What fast food franchise do you think will make it to Mars first? Are they all secretly there already, sponsoring your freeze dried, imported snacks and staples?

SMALL TALK

Zucchini Pancakes

2 medium zucchini, grated *(l)*
2 tbsp dehydrated onion *(i)*
½ cup egg (rehydrated or quail) *(i/l)*
8 tbsp oat flour *(l)*
1 tsp salt *(l)*
1 tbsp *oil (l)*

Mix grated zucchini, onion, oil, egg, baking powder and flour well.

Drop by spoonfuls onto hot, nonstick pan. When pancake is bubbled and the edges are just turning brown, flip them over to brown the other side.

Makes 10 pancakes

Do you have a recurring dream? Is there a particular piece you recognize every time, like a painting or a hallway with windows?

SMALL TALK

Candied Beets

3 tablespoons beet syrup *(l)*
1 tbsp butter powder *(i)*
3 cups thick sliced beet medallions *(l)*
1 tsp salt *(l)*
2 tbsp lemon juice (reconstituted) *(i)*

Place beet medallions in a dish with 2 tbsp water, cover and microwave until soft (5 min).

Combine beet sugar, lemon juice, butter and salt in a saucepan and cook until bubbling.

Add beets and continue to cook until liquid has fully evaporated and beets are left with a glaze.

Serves 6-8

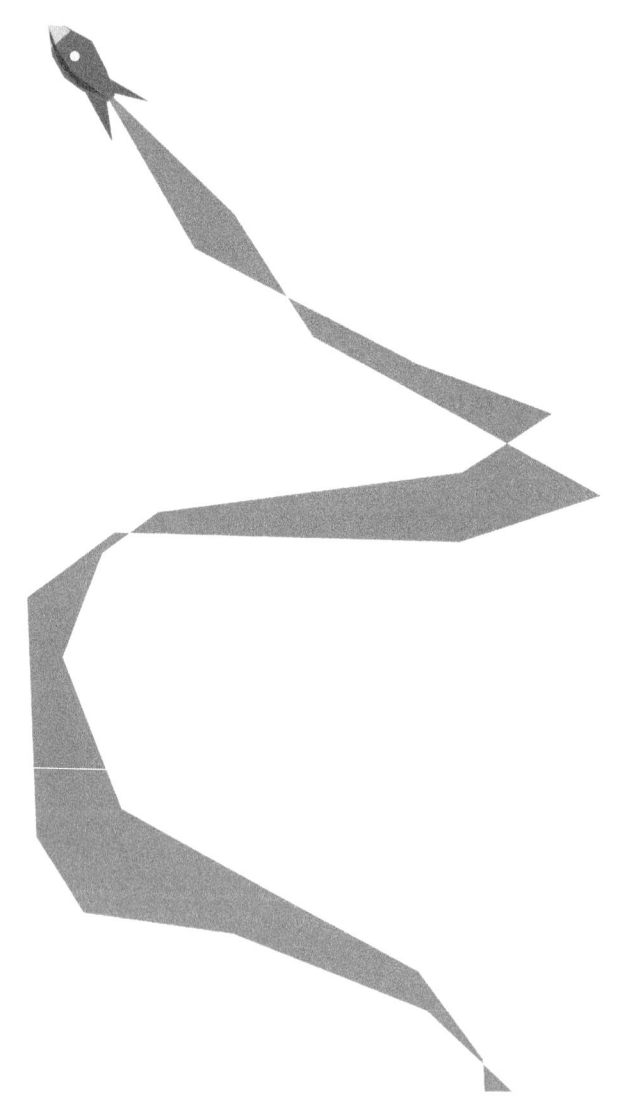

Tortillas

1 cup oat flour *(l)*
1 cup oilseed flour *(l)*
¼ cup butter (reconstituted) *(i)*
1 tbsp oil *(l)*
½ cup warm water *(l)*

Stir flours and salt together, then add in butter and mash with a fork until blended. Slowly add oil and stir until a dough forms.

Form dough into small, golf-ball sized balls. Roll out onto floured surface and pat between hands to shape.

Cook tortillas one at a time on a hot pan for around 30 seconds each or until they puff.

Serves 6-8

If you could learn a second, or third specialty, what would it be? How about a new language?

SMALL TALK

Beet Syrup

½ gallon chopped beets *(l)*
1 gallon water *(l)*
1 cup oilseed flour *(l)*
¼ cup butter (reconstituted) *(i)*
1 tbsp oil *(l)*
½ cup warm water *(l)*

Cover beets with water and boil until they are extremely mushy (60 min). Strain all of the solids out very well.

Return the liquid to heat and simmer. Skim the foam off as it forms.

Syrup will be ready when it "sheets" on the back of a spoon or the side of the pan.

Makes about 2 cups

What was your last thought before falling asleep last night?

SMALL TALK

Flour

6 cups pressed oilseed, oats or mealworms *(l)*

If using oilseed, be sure to use post-pressed seed. It will grind much better once the oil has been extracted.

If using mealworms, be sure they are fully roasted first.

Place chosen ingredient in grinder and run until a coarse flour is produced.

Makes about 6 cups flour

Have you started any new traditions since coming to Mars? If not, what tradition would you start if you could get everyone to go along?

SMALL TALK

Catsup

1 lb fresh tomatoes *(l)*
2 tbsp beet vinegar *(l)*
¼ tsp cinnamon *(i)*
¼ tsp salt *(i)*
¼ tsp mustard powder *(i)*
2 cup water *(l)*

Boil tomatoes for 5 minutes, then plunge into cold water. Remove the skin and seeds from the tomatoes. Squeeze tomatoes by hand and save juice for drinking.

Place squeezed tomatoes in pot and cover with water. Simmer until water is reduced by half and tomatoes form a smooth sauce.

Combine all ingredients and allow at least 12 hours for flavors to meld.

Makes about 2 cups

What was the last thing you had shipped over from Earth?

SMALL TALK

Sweet Potato Bread

½ cup sweet potato flesh, baked *(l)*
1 cup egg whites (reconstituted or quail) *(i/l)*
½ cup mealworm flour *(i)*
¼ cup oat flour *(i)*
1 tsp baking soda *(i)*

Mix all ingredients thoroughly and place in a loaf pan.

Bake at 350 for 30 minutes or until brown around the edges.

Makes 1 loaf

Beet Wine (part 1)

4 lbs chopped beets *(l)*
6 cups beet syrup *(l)*
½ cup beet vinegar *(l)*
1 1/2 cups cold, black tea *(i)*
1 tbsp oil *(l)*
1 packet wine yeast *(i)*

Two 1 gallon containers with a small mouth.
Airlock that fits your container.

Cover beets with water and boil until they are soft (30 min). Remove the beats for eating.

Add syrup and stir, then add vinegar, oil and tea. Stir well. Pour into a gallon container and add water until almost fill (leave room for ¼ cup).

Heat ¼ cup of water and add yeast. Stir well and allow to cool to room temperature. Add to gallon of beet mixture.

Cap with airlock and place in a warm place (around 70 degrees) for one week.

Beet Wine (part 2)

Have your second gallon container cleaned and ready.

After a week, move the liquid to a second gallon container. Leave behind any sediment that has settled to the bottom of the first container.

Place airlock on top of the new container and place jar back into the dark warm place for 8 weeks.

Drinkable wine takes time. It will be worth it, really.

After 8 weeks, decant your wine into smaller bottles/containers. Seal tightly and store in a cool dry place to finish fermenting for 4-6 months.

Makes about 1 gallon

Have you tried making up your own music? What do you use for instruments? Should Martian music have it's own, unique sound? What should it be called?

SMALL TALK

Beet Vinegar

1 tsp Mother of Vinegar *(i)*
1 cup fermented beet juice *(l)*

Glass jar/container *(i)*
Porous covering (cheesecloth or other) *(i)*

Place the Mother of Vinegar into the jar, then fill the jar to the brim with fermented beet juice.

Cover tightly with the cheesecloth and keep in a warm dark place until the jar smells strongly of vinegar (it will burn your nose strongly).

Strain off beet vinegar. Store the "Mother of Vinegar" (the slimy stuff on top) to make another batch later

Makes about 1 cup, depending on your jar.

What was the hardest new thing to learn this week? Did you finally get it, or are you still working on it?

SMALL TALK

Salsa

2 ripe tomatoes *(l)*
1 tbsp oil *(l)*
3 cups water *(l)*
1 dried ancho chili (seeds removed) *(i)*
1 tsp beet vinegar *(l)*
1 tsp garlic powder *(i)*
Salt *(l)*

Remove seeds, then coat tomatoes lightly with oil and roast until they start to char in spots. Remove and allow to cool.

Boil water and add garlic and the ancho chili. Cook about 5 minutes, then remove the chili and save ¼ cup of the water.

Add all ingredients to the reserved liquid and blend until smooth.

Makes about 1 cup

DEHYDRATED FOODS

A great many foods will likely be shipped in a dehydrated form. This removes almost all of the water from a food, which makes it lightweight and, if properly packaged, gives it a shelf-life that lasts for decades. Most of the nutrients present in the food are considered to remain intact through the process, which means that, once they have been reconstituted, they are just as healthy (and often as good-looking) as they were when fresh.

Many dehydrated foods can be eaten just as they are, as crunchy snacks, and in fact this is one of the most common ways to find them sold, particularly fruits like apples, strawberries and bananas. Just be sure you drink a lot of water.

When cooking with dehydrated foods, you want to restore them to as close as their original condition as possibly. This means taking the time to rehydrate them properly. You want to use a 1 to 1 ratio when rehydrating foods like vegetables or fruits for cooking. This means 1 cup of water for every 1 cup of dehydrated product.

You can rehydrate using either warm or cold water. It's recommended that you use the water that suits your dish (so if you will be boiling everything in the next few steps, go ahead and use hot water, but if you are going to be baking or sautéing, then cold water might be your go-to).

Just remember, if you are going to be using hot water, don't allow your rehydrated foods to stand for too long, and when you do use them, be sure to get the dish to a full boil or at least 350 degrees, just in case any bacteria decided to take up residence in the meantime.

As an added bonus, Mars has a very dry, very cold atmosphere. Almost perfect for natural freeze drying. Leftover foods can be packaged and stored outside the habitat for preservation (since attracting scavengers like bears and raccoons is extremely unlikely).

ALTITUDE ISSUES

Even if we decide that it is an ethical choice to terraform Mars, that process that will take hundreds of years (assuming we get the math right on the first try). Humans who colonize the red planet are going to start out so living in atmospherically controlled habitats, where the air pressure and temperature are being handled for the good of the overall colony, rather than the soufflé you have baking in your oven.

There are a number of factors that will govern the atmospheric pressure levels inside the Martian habitats, not just at the outset, when facilities are being constructed, but as the habitat evolves over time, changes may need to be made in order to reduce the time to acclimate to an EVA suit (for trips outside the habitat) or the ability to move back and forth between greenhouses, insect farms and working quarters.

It is not beyond reason that the atmosphere inside the habitat is at either a lower or higher pressure than sea-level on Earth, nor is it implausible that the lesser gravity on Mars might play a role in how breads rise or protein bars compact. The comparatively slight difference in air-pressure between San Diego and Aspen is enough to wreck your holiday dinner plans, and compared to the much larger possible variances in atmosphere (the Apollo missions were conducted at 5psi, or roughly 1/3 Earth atmosphere, whereas our current missions on the ISS are conducted at 15 psi or one Earth atmosphere).

This is only of those aspects that is going to have to evolve over time. We can provide guidelines, for example; if your muffins dip in the middle, you may need to add vinegar to the baking soda to give it a boost. Experienced chefs learn to account for these things very quickly. Maybe the new oven has a warm spot in the back, or your pancakes don't come out of the pan smoothly on days when it's raining. Being able to cook on a daily basis means you have to be flexible, and you have to understand (even unconsciously) the relationships between your ingredients, the cooking process you are using and, yes, even how high up the mountain you are.

Air pressure issues are going to be most obvious when preparing dishes that require some kind of leavening (like baking soda or baking powder) so for the purposes of this cookbook, I have tried to steer clear of recipes that require such things. Other foods are going to be affected as well, water will evaporate at a different rate, which will affect verying levels of "done-ness" for most kinds of food. On Earth, you usually just do the best you can and stomach the result, but on Mars, adjustments are going to have to be made either to the food preparation or our expectations as to what that food will look, taste and feel like. I am including some suggestions here for both low and high-altitude adjustments.

ALTITUDE ADJUSTMENTS

1. **Pressure.** Check your psi every so often. Ideally an off-planet habitat (Martian or otherwise) will be kept around sea-level pressure (or 15 psi). Keep in mind that changes in pressure as small as .5 psi can affect cooking times and techniques.

2. **Boiling point.** The length of time it takes for water to boil increases (or decreases) by about 2 degrees for every 1,000 ft.

3. **Evaporation.** Water evaporates more quickly at a higher psi. This means that cooking techniques that rely on the removal of water (braising, baking) will require additional liquid.

4. **Leavening.** The structure and texture of cakes, muffins, breads, even tortillas all depend on air cells created by leavening products (baking powder/soda). If the air pressure is low, these cells can grow too large too fast. If the air pressure is higher, the cells will not grow large enough.

5. **Cook times.** For some techniques, you will need to adjust your cooking times, but for non-bakery foods cooked in the oven, the usual times should be effective.

NOTES ON HUSBANDRY

One might question the decision to take different species of animals to Mars. Mars, after all, has no life of its own that we have been able to find. In order to maintain and develop a healthy ecosystem, we need to have diversity. Monoculture, the farming practice of producing only a single crop, historically develops serious problems over time. Growing one particular type of plant in a particular area over and over depletes the soil, it makes successive harvests lower in yield and lower in nutrient value. We are going to need to make sure that we include a broad variety of life.

Ideally, harvests and growth cycles will be planned so that once one plant takes nutrients from the soil, the next planting will be of a plant that either removes different nutrients or puts back at nutrients so that we can continue the cycle. Rotational farming is a well-established practice, and plans should absolutely be put in place to help maintain top-quality, nutrient rich soil for the purposes of feeding our colonists.

While this particular book focuses on the edibles, we will need a range of plants and animals that all contribute to a local ecosystem with a minimum of important minerals, bacteria and chemicals that might have to be brought all the way from Earth.

As an example, the cuy that I have proposed as a protein source, should some of the colonists decide they prefer a vegetarian diet, they still serve a purpose. Their poop helps to fix nitrogen in the soil, which makes it available to plants, they can take waste plant matter, for example the stems and stocks of the oil seed plants, and turn them back into bio-matter that can be used to nourish other plants. Far from being a useful only as a tasty comestible, every creature, every plant brought along will have a job or multiple jobs to do.

It will be our first opportunity to truly bioengineer a functional, working ecosystem. One specifically tailored to the needs of a human colony.

THE NEW ECOLOGY

Mars is a dead world. We like to give it life in our minds, in our stories, but the fact of the matter is that we are looking at a planet that is, currently, incapable of sustaining life on its own. It hardly seems fair. It's a perfectly good planet, right in the goldilocks zone, still maintains some modicum of atmosphere, has water hidden under the surface that we, as the clever creatures we are, will figure out how to make use of pretty darned quickly.

In order to make life work, in order to colonize our sister planet, we are going to need to build our own bubbles, our own habitable spaces and thrive within those. This means we are going to have to take the time and effort to develop our own biomes, our own mini-ecologies. It's not enough to drop some poop into the dirt and voila, we can grow things. In order to have a sustainable farming situation we will need to not only add bacteria and nutrients to the dirt to make soil, but we will need to add worms to help aerate, we will need to select plants that not only take nutrients, but who can give back as well. Modified versions of rotational crop planting will likely come into play. Since the surface of Mars has no natural scavengers or predators, food storage is an easy thing to manage, the outside atmosphere is essentially one giant, hardcore refrigerator.

Right now, at least for the early missions, NASA figures that it will actually be cheaper to ship foodstuffs to Mars than it will be to ship all the materials we need to farm successfully, at least in the short term. This makes perfect sense for the types of scientific missions we plan to run in the beginning. Eventually though, we're going to start looking and developing a self-sustaining system. To do this, we don't need to send over 10,000 people in one shot and start large-scale farming operations. We can start with 10 and supplement their freeze-dried comestibles with fresh produce, developing technologies and techniques suited to farming on Martian soil. Next we make the jump to 100 people and continue to expand farming capabilities, going from what essentially would be a family-sized doomsday-prepper garden to something more like a community plot. From there we can continue to expand slowly, meeting the needs of the colony first and evolving the tools and experience we need for larger-scale food production.

REFERENCES

Bastiaens, F.G. *Oilseed Flour for Human Food*. Journal of the American Oil Chemists' Society. 53: 6 (1976)

Matthews, Ruth H., Sharpe, Elinora J. and Clark, Willa M. *The Use of Some Oilseed Flours in Bread*. Human Nutrition Research Division, Agricultural Research Service. 47: 181 (1970)

Wamelink GWW, Frissel JY, Krijnen WHJ, Verwoert MR, Goedhart PW. *Can Plants Grow on Mars and the Moon: A Growth Experiment on Mars and Moon Soil Simulants.* PLoS ONE 9(8): e103138. doi:10.1371/journal.pone.0103138 (2014)

Quarters, C. *The Best Vegetables to Grow Hydroponically*. Demand Media, SFGate Home Guides: Web Article www.sfgate.com (2015).

Oko, D. *On the Long Trip to Mars, What Will the Astronauts Eat?* Houston Chronicle: Web Article www.houstonchronicle.com (2014).

Adams, P. *This is the Food We'll Eat on Mars: A crew of scientists and astronauts prepare to feed human colonists on the red planet.* PopSci: Web Article www.popsci.com (2012)

LaVone, M. *The Future of Food on Mars.* SpaceSafetyMagazine: Web Article www.spacesafetymagazine.com (2014)

Herridge, L. *Veggie Plant Growth Systems Activated on International Space Station*. NASA: Web Article www.nasa.gov (2014).

Associated Press. *In Space, Nobody Likes the Ice Cream (but Astronauts will cook fresh vegetables on Mars): The NASA Scientists Preparing Food for a Three-Year Mission to the Red Planet*. Daily Mail: Web Article www.dailymail.co.uk (2012)

Bland, A. From Pets to Plates: *Why More People are Eating Guinea Pigs*. NPR: Food for Thought Web Article www.npr.com (2013)

Li, C.Y., Maser, C., Maser, Z. and Caldwell, B.A. *Role of Three Rodents in Forest Nitrogen Fixation in Western Oregon: Another Aspect of Mammal-Mycorrhizal Fungus-Tree Mutualism*. Great Basin Naturalist. 46: 3 (1986)

Lane, H. W.; Feeback, D. L. *History of nutrition in space flight. Nutrition* **18** (10): 797–804 (2002).

Perchonok, M; Douglas, G; Cooper, M. *Risk of Performance Decrement and Crew Illness Due to an Inadequate Food System*. Johnson Space Center, Houston: National Aeronautics and Space Administration, Lyndon B. Johnson Space Center. pp. 4–5 (2009).

McPhee, J; Charles, J. *Human health and performance risks of space exploration missions : evidence reviewed by the NASA Human Research Program* (PDF). Johnson Space Center, Houston: National Aeronautics and Space Administration, Lyndon B. Johnson Space Center. pp. 4–5

ACKNOWDLEGEMENTS

There are a handful of people in my life who always say "YES! DO THE THING!" and to those people I will be forever grateful. Even when I don't do the THING, whatever crazy idea that thing might be or might have been, I know that they will have my back no matter what. This book was just such a THING. So Marc, Antoinette, Jared, Rich, Warren, Lissa, Marc (the evil twin one), thank you.

To Mom, who instilled in me (quite accidentally) a love of the artistry of the cookbook. No, I still won't eat my broccoli, no matter how pretty the pictures are.

ABOUT THE AUTHOR

"Food saves, food destroys, there is no enemy like food." -Marathi Proverb

Margaret Ellory has a long-running relationship with food. Sometimes it's a good one, sometimes they fight like sisters over the last pot-brownie. Couple with this a lifelong love of science-fiction, the daily necessity of making meatloaf interesting for three kids and a spouse, and you have a mealtime richly imbued with a host of "what if's" and "why that's" and "OMG, you can EAT THAT?".

www.ingramcontent.com/pod-product-compliance
Lightning Source LLC
Chambersburg PA
CBHW050542300426
44113CB00012B/2224